Super Safari 1

Student's Book

Herbert Puchta   **Günter Gerngross**   **Peter Lewis-Jones**

CAMBRIDGE
UNIVERSITY PRESS

Map of the book

Hello! (pages 4–7)

Vocabulary	Chant: Grammar
Gina, Polly, Leo, Mike	Hello! I'm (Jo).

▶ **Total physical response:** Stand up, sit down, say "hello"	▶ **Song:** Hello!

1 My class (pages 8–15)

Vocabulary	Chant: Grammar	Story and value	CLIL	Thinking skills
bag, pencil, book, chair	Look! It's my (chair).	*The chair* Saying *sorry*	School behavior	Classifying

▶ **Total physical response:** Hands up, hands down, clap your hands	▶ **Song:** In the classroom

2 My colors (pages 16–23)

Vocabulary	Chant: Grammar	Story and value	CLIL	Thinking skills
red, blue, green, yellow	It's (yellow).	*The painters* Cheering someone up	Rainbow colors	Testing predictions

▶ **Total physical response:** Show me something red, show me something green, show me something yellow	▶ **Song:** Stand up and paint with me!

3 My family (pages 24–31)

Vocabulary	Chant: Grammar	Story and value	CLIL	Thinking skills
dad, mom, brother, sister	Who's this?	*Family and friends* Caring about family and friends	Understanding age	Ordering

▶ **Total physical response:** Go to sleep, wake up, give your dad a hug	▶ **Song:** Rosemary, Rosemary

4 My toys (pages 32–39)

Vocabulary	Chant: Grammar	Story and value	CLIL	Thinking skills
ball, car, puzzle, doll	I have a (car).	*The puzzle* Helping	Big and small	Sorting

▶ **Total physical response:** Throw your ball, catch your ball, oh, no, clean up	▶ **Song:** I have a ball

5 My numbers (pages 40–47)

Vocabulary one, two, three, four	Chant: Grammar one book, two books	Story and value *Where's Polly?* Playing together	CLIL Quantity	Thinking skills Describing with numbers

▶ **Total physical response:** Four, three, two, one   ▶ **Song:** Sing some more

6 My pets (pages 48–55)

Vocabulary bird, rabbit, fish, cat	Chant: Grammar What is it?	Story and value *The cat* Working as a team	CLIL Species	Thinking skills Making deductions

▶ **Total physical response:** Jump, walk, fly, swim   ▶ **Song:** What is this?

7 My food (pages 56–63)

Vocabulary pasta, salad, rice, cake	Chant: Grammar I like (rice).	Story and value *The cake* Sharing	CLIL Solids and liquids	Thinking skills Focusing on detail

▶ **Total physical response:** Look! Pasta, eat the pasta, it's yummy, wash your face   ▶ **Song:** I like yummy lunch!

8 My clothes (pages 64–71)

Vocabulary T-shirt, pants, dress, shoes	Chant: Grammar I don't like (the purple dress).	Story and value *The party* Including your friends	CLIL Wearing a costume	Thinking skills Categorizing

▶ **Total physical response:** Put on the shoes, put on a T-shirt, put on a hat, say "hello" to your dad   ▶ **Song:** Clothes

9 My park (pages 72–79)

Vocabulary slide, merry-go-round, seesaw, swing	Chant: Grammar The (swing)'s fun.	Story and value *The park* Taking turns	CLIL Circles and triangles	Thinking skills Sequencing

▶ **Total physical response:** Sit down on the seesaw, down you go, up you go, oh, no   ▶ **Song:** Let's go to the park

Phonics (pages 80–89)

Unit 1: "p" pencil	Unit 2: "b" bag	Unit 3: "d" dad	Unit 4: "c" car	Unit 5: "t" two	Unit 6: "e" eggs	Unit 7: "s" salad	Unit 8: "n" nose	Unit 9: "i" igloo	Phonics review

 pages 90–94   **Certificate:** 95   **Stickers:** End section

 www.cambridge.org/supersafari/familyfun

Hello!

1 CD1 02 **Listen and point. Say the names.**

Gina, Polly, Leo, Mike

2 Listen and chant.

Family fun!   Hello! I'm (Jo).   5

3 CD1 04 Listen and act.

4 Listen and sing.

1 My class

1 CD1 08 **Listen and point. Say the words.**

8 bag, pencil, book, chair

2 CD1 09 Listen and trace. Chant.

Family fun!

Look! It's my (chair).

9

Listen and act.

4 CD1 13 14 **Listen and sing.**

1

2

3

4

School behavior

 6 Listen and point. Say the words.

7 (Think!) **Look and complete the faces.**

1

2

Thinking skills: Classifying   **15**

2 My colors

1 🔊 CD1 20 **Listen and point. Say the colors.**

red, blue, green, yellow

2 CD1 21 **Listen and color. Chant.**

3 Listen and act. Listen and color.

CD1 22 23

1   2   3

Total physical response

4 CD1 25 26 **Listen and sing.**

Family fun!

The painters

Family fun!

Rainbow colors

6 **Listen and point. Say the colors.**

7 (Think!) **Look and say the colors. Color.**

Thinking skills: Testing predictions   **23**

3 My family

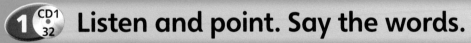

1 CD1 32 Listen and point. Say the words.

dad, mom, brother, sister

2 CD1 33 Listen and trace. Chant.

1

2

3

4

1 2 3

4 CD1 37 38 **Listen and sing.**

Family and friends

Animal families

6 CD1 42 **Listen and point. Trace and say the words.**

7 (Think!) **Follow the path.**

(Thinking skills: Ordering) **31**

4 My toys

1 CD1 45 **Listen and point. Say the toys.**

 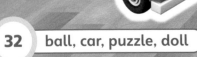

2 CD1 47 Listen and match. Chant.

1

2

3

3 Listen and act. Listen and color.

1

2

3

4

Total physical response

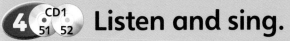

4 Listen and sing.

CD1 51 52

Family fun!

Singing for fun 35

The puzzle

1

2

3

4

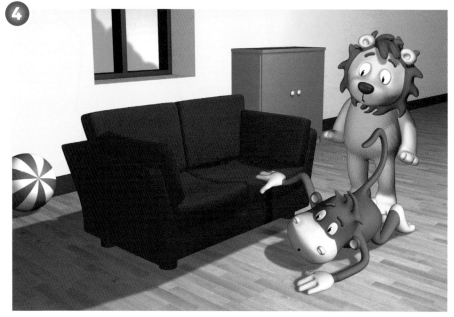

Big and small

Listen and point. Trace and say the words.

1

2

3

4

5

6

7 **Think!** Look and draw lines. Say "big" or "small".

5 My numbers

1 CD2 02 **Listen and point. Say the numbers.**

2 CD2 04 **Listen and match. Chant.**

1

2

3

4

Family fun!

one book, two books **41**

3 Listen and act. Listen and color.

1

2

3

4

Total physical response

4 CD2 08 09 **Listen and sing.**

5

Family fun!

Singing for fun 43

Sticker

Values

Quantity

Listen and point. Trace and say the numbers.

7 (Think!) **Look and match. Say the numbers.**

1 2 3 4

Thinking skills: Describing with numbers   47

6 My pets

1 CD2 16 Listen and point. Say the pets.

bird, rabbit, fish, cat

2 CD2 17 Listen and color. Chant.

3 CD2 19 20 **Listen and act. Listen and color.**

4 CD2 22 23 **Listen and sing.**

The cat

1

2

3

4

Species

6 **CD2 26** Listen and point. Draw lines and say.

1

2

3

7 (Think!) **Look and say the words.**

1

2

3

4

(Thinking skills: Making deductions) **55**

7 My food

1 CD2 28 **Listen and point. Say the food.**

pasta, salad, rice, cake

2 CD2 29 Listen and trace. Chant.

1

2

3

4

Family fun!

I like (rice). 57

3 Listen and act. Listen and color.

CD2 30 31

4 CD2 33 34 **Listen and sing.**

The cake

Value: Sharing 61

Solids and liquids

1

2

3

4

7 Think! **Look and match.**

1
2
3
4

Thinking skills: Focusing on detail   **63**

8 My clothes

1 CD2 40 **Listen and point. Say the clothes.**

2 CD2 41 Listen and color. Chant.

Family fun!

I don't like (the purple dress). 65

3 Listen and act. Listen and color.

1

2

3

4

Total physical response

4 CD2 46 47 **Listen and sing.**

Value: Including your friends

Wearing a costume

Listen and point. Trace and say the words.

1

2

3

7 Think! **Circle the clothes.**

Thinking skills: Categorizing   **71**

⑨ My park

1 CD2 52 Listen and point. Say the words.

slide, merry-go-round, seesaw, swing

2 CD2 54 Listen and match. Chant.

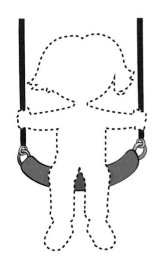

Family fun!

The (swing)'s fun. 73

3 Listen and act. Listen and color.

CD2 56 57

Total physical response

4 CD2 59 60 **Listen and sing.**

Family fun!

The park

Values

Value: Taking turns

Circles and triangles

 6 **Listen and point. Count and say the shapes.**

7 (Think!) **Look and draw lines. Say the shapes.**

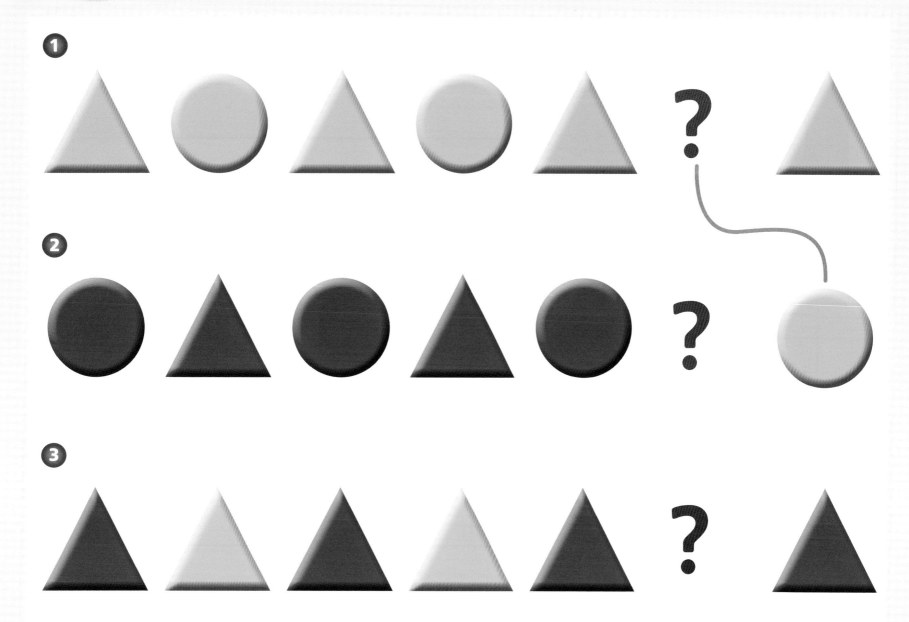

(Thinking skills: Sequencing) **79**

1 Look and find.

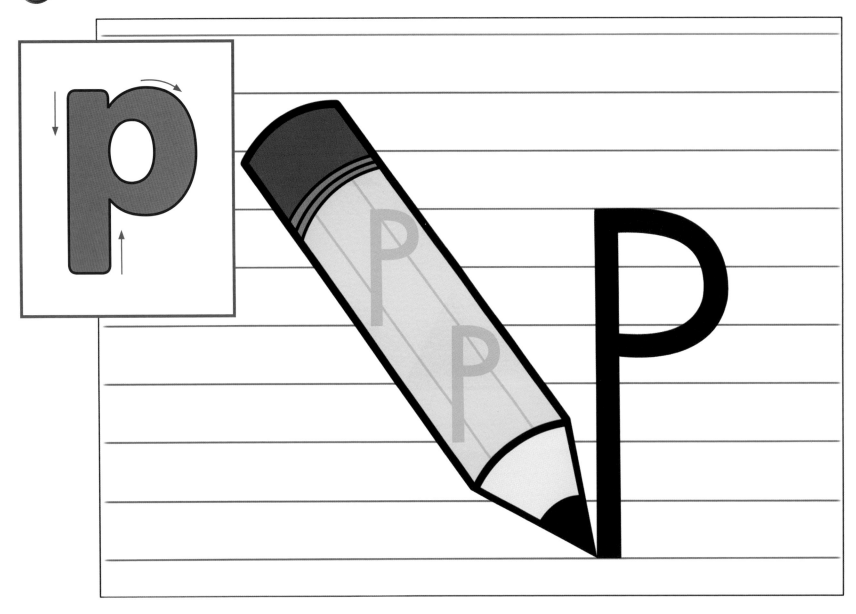

2 CD1 18 Listen and join in.

1 Look and find.

2 CD1 31 Listen and join in.

1 Look and find.

1 Look and find. Color the letter.

2 (CD1 57) Listen and join in.

1 Look and find. Color the letter.

2 CD2 14 Listen and join in.

1 Look and find. Color the letter.

2 CD2 27 Listen and join in.

1 Look and find. Trace the letter.

1 Look and find. Trace the letter.

2 CD2 51 Listen and join in.

1 Look and find. Trace the letter.

Listen and play bingo.

1 **Listen to the sentences. Color the frames.**

1 Listen and color the circles. Color the frames.

  Review

Unit 2 & Unit 3 **91**

Listen and color the circles. Color the frames.

Listen and color the circles. Color the frames.

1 🔘 CD2 65 Listen and color the circles. Color the frames.